The Seed Is Waiting in the Dark

poems by

Meesha Goldberg

Finishing Line Press
Georgetown, Kentucky

The Seed Is Waiting in the Dark

ACKNOWLEDGMENTS

Variations of "Roadkill", "Imagine Circles", and "Survival" first appeared in
Mala Leche

Publisher: Leah Huete de Maines
Editor: Christen Kincaid
Cover Art: Meesha Goldberg
Author Photo: Kori Price
Cover Design: Elizabeth Maines McCleavy

Order online: www.finishinglinepress.com
also available on amazon.com

Author inquiries and mail orders:
Finishing Line Press
PO Box 1626
Georgetown, Kentucky 40324
USA

Contents

Spawn

If I open my mouth
maybe
a south by southeast prayer
might fly
might finish this melody
begun in my gut

In my gut
are a hundred fish
ready to spawn up a river
missing her indigenous name

My name was once in my mother's mouth
My name was once in my mother tongue
My tongue is forked
at the bend where a hundred fish
swim upriver to spawn

My name is dammed
Her name was *Kyong*
If I open my mouth
maybe the name of the river
might spill
out

Folk Poem

This is a folk poem
a simple poem
It belongs to the people
It belongs to the fire
It was made to ignite
the burdened spirit
Its words embroider
our common desire
stitch by stitch
with blackbirds

This is a folk poem
it belongs to the water
No one owns the water
No one owns the spirit
The poem is a seed
in the field of the people
Who knows what can grow
with a little fire

A simple poem
is a good poem
A good poem
belongs to the earth
A folk poem comes in
with the harvest
A folk poem
is simple like corn

It was grown to feed
the hungry spirit
It belongs to the air
It spreads on the wind
Whatever the need
the folk poem blooms
as a weed
with humble medicine

Good

I'm trying to imagine a time
when like deer
we wandered into a valley
& it was good
The water ran clear
We built a fire for the night
& stayed awhile
We put a seed in the ground
We put our bones in the ground
Before
the water ran clear

I'm trying to imagine a time
when it was kind
& our seeds grew from joyful bones
We could breathe the air
We could literally breathe the air
The soul was good
so we built a body out of songs
& stayed awhile
The water ran clear
We could drink
bowed down to it
as deer

Was there ever a time
when it was good?

Because the sky's instinct is beauty
because walking the trail of the deer
fills us with sky
good must be imminent

The seed is waiting in the dark
The seed is waiting for water
or maybe fire to open

If ever that time was or is to be
I reckon it'd be there, in the passage
of clear water running through the earth

Roadkill

Laid over with serpentine roads
the Earth hums with combustion
Machines swarm
The colony incessantly roves
locked into routine
to work & back to the nest
headlights beaming

Watch out if you follow the herd
or fly low
The road is a graveyard
See them flat or neck askew
in a shroud of vultures
returning to the sky

Especially when the leaves golden
& the bucks lose their minds
on the scent of the doe
you see them strewn & supine
kept cold on the approach of solstice
So like coyotes we drag our haul
& hoist the bodies in the back of the truck
when there's a break in the traffic

The Earth is made of food
We are one another's harvest
So take your knife & basket
& gather on the low branch, the bramble
the roots & leaves of common weeds
Reel in from clear waters & roadsides
where the freshly slaughtered
just leapt out the pure woods & into metal
like a bullet

We bring the deer to the hilltop
to gut, for the eagles to lunch
where the ancient blue mountains

surround & watch
Opening the body you think
of the self, gone
though the blood is still warm
You thank the deer & her kin
for the body you live in
then take limb by limb
& tenderloin along the backbone
leaving the rest for the wilderness

Nature wastes not
& so living by nature's law
we scavenge casualties
of the Anthropocene
feasting but not having to kill
animal eating animal
our blood running together
wild & white tailed

7

Daughterland Ritual Poem

On September 7th, 2021, I walked for thirteen hours
encircling an ancient oak tree in Virginia to honor my
mother/Earth

I'm just gonna hold
this mirror up
for a good look behind me

because you've got to know
the body is a pair
of haunted shoes

Maybe I'll get myself some healing
seeking language
of wildwood

but until then I'll just
circle here
uncircling

See these bloodlines of mine
crisscross at crossroads
all mixed up off mountains

but now I'm the judge
sorting the yellow girl from white
with the red white blues

because way back when
my mama got up
& left the motherland

with a green army man—oh
GI bride, war baby
you got out the country alive

Now they call the Korean War
the Forgotten War
just a four million slaughter

Back then they catcalled
the GI bride
a yankee whore

but you know the body
is a ledger
keeping score

& until these soles are good & calloused
I think I'll circle here
uncircling

Circle here barefoot
on red land on Monacan ground
Aeons

of ancestors
mounded
now gone ploughed

I'm just gonna call my body
the Daughterland now
because back where

was napalmed
& high rised
& all these homes

are haunted &
camouflaged white
But oh

the swansong
of wildwood turns me on
& I'm in love

with an ancient oak
who's gone dodged
every European

She ain't my elder
but maybe she'll help me
find my tongue

Mothertree
may I enshrine you
in white ribbon?

My mama wrote me a diary
in her dying year
at thirty-eight

I'm wearing it now
as a rice white gown
to celebrate

She wrote
How long I will live
everything I cannot predict

This time
This moment
I guess I can only live today

So today
I'll just circle here
uncircling here

Now is my moment
This time I'm thirty-eight
I guess today is our

38th parallel
I guess this moment
is our parallel fate

& I guess this tree
is our
DMZ

A matriarchal vibration
must remain down
in the root

Somewhere
there's an ambered echo
to retrieve

a feeling
like the grace of hands
braiding the hair of kinfolk

whose hands braid
the hair of kin
braiding hair

down
the spine of generations
black silk black kink

The war was never ended
so all can't yet
be lost

& so I'm going off
journeying then
barefoot in the Daughterland

patient for sacred medicine
circling, uncircling
& circling again

like a moon
or maybe
a buzzard

in the presence
of the ancestors
walking for my mother

who wrote, *Love is*
while we live together
in this world

something
more essential
than air

Survival

1.

You lived in this way since Creator
sung you to life—
surviving by the generous Earth

You were made of the ground
you died upon

Dreams gave you the songs
you had the stillness to hear

You endured in the circle
of elders and children

Death was kin

You killed & prayed
& washed the blood in the river

You spoke the language of the sky

2.

These days, ancestors
I saw & haul
split & light
feast & fast
carry the seeds
wash the roots
honor the fish & doe
share the warm feeling
as the sun & fire

Thank you for showing me
the sun in the fire
Thank you for clarifying
medicine from poison

If women's tears
are healing rain
there must be grief enough
for our vision to return
& the forest to welcome us home

By this flood of pain
may we be purified
to endure

3.

Listen, child
why were you given ears?

Don't you feel the ache in the sea?
Don't you even know how to feel?

How can you gut your Mother's lungs?
How can you subtract your Mother's birds?

Burn your green paper culture
you've forgotten what you are

That rank west wind is the extinction
That silence is the generations

There are not vultures enough
There are not tears enough

All this green flourish & fruiting
all my blue & this Turtle Island

The shriek of Her furnace
Her merciless skies

will humble you
Humanity, too, is disposable

You don't even know, child
You don't even know how to survive

Salt

Do not tell me the weeping world
     should not flood
          these decaying streets in salt enough
               to make real grief's sting

There are so many scars in the sky
     tonight
          going supernova
               you could not count them all

but could you
     this moment
          trace a constellation
               between wounds?

Shake this salt on your words
     Shake your words off your tongue
          Do not tell me that time & silence
               will deform us less than

                    unrelenting witness

Standing Rock

Circled overhead like prey—
helicopters imitated eagles
snipers thought themselves human
police played white horse cowboy
pow pow pow
vs. the indians

Fires defied blizzards
guns fired at song
& beneath even the bones
oil, Earth's memory
ran black in the psychic rock
To extract is to forget
& neglect the prophetic

Each dawn prayer rang through ancient light
& spoke, *Remember why you're here*
The drum woke up the human within
The river washed American harm
There is no peace if we are not all healed
We prayed even for the CEO's
& politician's children

Gold

They don't deserve
forgiveness, no
these villains
seeding sorrow
building strongholds
in the country of our thoughts
Like a virus they've even
infected this verse
but see us blackbirds
chasing down the hawk

They've rewrote our seeds
& patented the crops
They don't deserve
an audience, no
but here the villains ride in
dominating the scene
seeding sorrow
from great storehouses of pain
all too generously

Strike the match

When the reigning villain
broadcasts his seed
women clamp your legs
as Mother Nature
clenches her clouds
in drought
& closes her furrowed fields
in defense

Burn the screens
propagating abominations
of the Real

Everything they say
I reverse
to translate truth
Every truth I've earned
was a long long walk
to find alone
Every time my compassion
rusts to rage
I see our wound

the bone we broke
when we fell from grace

They don't deserve
the water of women
or the bed of green spring
to bring them home
but the fevered gluttons
must be given all they want
everything
even the gold
even the gold of forgiveness

Thank you brother, thank you
that we may plough down
to even this unlikely depth

The Sweet Potato Man

The red earth wants red root
She breaks & opens in furrows & in hills
If you know how to work the dirt
she'll set your table
serve up a year of meals

root in me baby
root in me all evenin long
i'll grow for you baby
grow for you all summer long
just give me some thunder
& a sweet potato song

There was a sweet potato man, south of Orange down Route 3
had a little roadside stand off a quarter acre plot
had ninety-nine years working the red earth
Oh he grew food back when you'd ride a horse to town

It wasn't no secret how to grow gold
but the old country folk don't pass it down in books
They're back there hacking a handle from a respectable oak
figuring out a tool that'll make work easier

like the sweet potato stick, carved sharp, hip high
with a hand's length cross piece nailed off to one side
& eight inches off the point so you can pierce the row
& measure the depth & space between the planting holes

root in me baby
root in me all evenin through
i'll feed you plenty honey
feed you past the seasons through
just give me a lil lightning
sing those sweet potato blues

Come spring he'd take the best off last year's crop
to the house & into some dirt to sprout
The first of the vine coming off each eye
got buried in the garden to multiply

So between sunset & moonrise, after last frost & before the rain
we go bow down again & again planting sprouts on down the row
bowing down to the miracle begun underground
till fireflies spark in the poplar grove

like the spirits of all the long gone sweet men
suspended somewhere between heaven & hills of earth
looking over our crop through summer & past equinox
Better get em dug out before first frost!

The red earth wants red root
The red earth wants green songs
soil tilled in with plenty rot
gonna grow a hundred bushels for the pot
If you gotta good patch of dirt
Mother Nature'll do the rest of the work

Farm Wife

Each morning she is given
the gold ring of the sun

By night she is given silver

After new moon, then
a sliver crescent sickle
laying down
the western wheat field

The land demands devotion
as a man

I do, she says, each dawn

It don't take long to dissolve
to dream each night

I do, again, by birdsong
or by rooster
if she keeps him from the fox

Always, peace pendulums

Thunder floods what blue parches

Green will pattern the quilt of the valley
till the hills barren
& it's time to hay the herd

It would all go to wilderness
if not for a lot of tenderness
& a fence

The vining weeds tangle
as the caterpillars fatten

Look away
& the hawk takes the head
of the hen

The farm wife is wed to the earth
as the bee belongs to her hive
Love requires work to last past harvest
Work requires love to survive

So she stacks the pantry
with the season's fruits
as the bee seals spring
within the comb

It'd all be much too much work
without the sweetness

Winter wipes the green slate clean
as the sap descends to the root
Till death do us part, the farm wife says
leaning against her scythe

Quiet!

A jar—sunflower, cattail, rose
A hand—coin, hand, salt

A woman—wait
for her, she does not know

what is inside
Wheat, wind, sun

Hands
milk

beginnings
Quiet!

She does not yet know
she is being exceeded

Look how gently she sleeps while dreaming
of tidal waves

An ocean—whale
water, salt

She performs
her daily tasks—washes her hair

prepares
meals, thinks aloud

replies, *Fine*
& you?

By now
the child has grown its heart

Magnolia womb
Equinox

For her sake, let us not
prolong irony

A mother—
she is growing

suspicious of her
microcosmos

Her lover, too
wonders at her swollen breasts

as he delights in them
The bud

unfurls
A mother—

tidal, child
herself

Snap!
Tomorrow

she will discover the child
but until then

observe how sincerely
she thinks only of herself

The Body Alone

Leaves lean into sunlight, the hungry
into the redolence of food, the wolf into the warmth of fur
& the seed, too, leans into the soil
Leaning is the most basic of motions
The body alone is a fragile vial

This may be called gravity
This may be called instinct
There is no word that does not lean into meaning
Only the joshua tree is of desert hermitage

I lean into him because love is hunger. The snake
bathes on the stone because heat is life
The moon leans toward Earth, oceans toward moon
He leans into me because love is heat

After many days where I do not bleed, I lean over
the test—a blue cross for yes, a blue line for no one
As the cross appears I lean into the future
The cross appears and someone leans into my womb

In winter, the hemisphere leans away from the sun
In drought, water leans away from the ground
In war, gods lean away from their creation
& the mother, too,
leans away

Knowledge

What did my mother know
that there was not time to teach?
What did she learn from her mother
that is forever gone?
Who cut the generations
& collaged us around the world?

I guess it was our fate
to never be at home
Now when a root wants water
it walks off to other soil

Did my mother know
what our ancestors knew—

the plants that healed the wound

the prayer to sing by bones

where water seeps out the ground

how to think beyond
one lifetime?

Almost gone, almost gone
but for the instinct beneath my name
that can still smell out the water

Though daughterless
at least
I learn the plants that heal the wound

Motivation

We imagined our relatives
still put us anonymously into prayers
on lunar new year, but there was
no telling. There was no telling
if our ancestors would descend
eighteen hours
just to reach us speaking English
In the fiction of a new world
we fragmented our longing
but as we are mountainless
in that wound
imagination festered
Nothing suggested such
but we imagined ourselves
remembered
& that myth's sore legs
could walk us

Our American cloud mountain, Septembered
& berried
We imagined how grandmothers could guide us
the blindfolded
though we did not offer a single persimmon
though wild tigers stalked us out of our dreams
though we ripped out every root with great carelessness
our longing is holy
because we did not abandon it

All ginseng gatherers 심마니 feel the same
if they don't find any for a couple days
They feel the urge to give up
That's when the mountain spirit gives you one
That's what motivates us to keep going

Imagine Circles

The way the old walnut spreads a feast
circled round its feet
The way the chestnut feeds us
up through till solstice light
The way the oak offers mushrooms
through death returned to life
The way the wild foods spring the wild in I
The way spring returns all things to green

By rings & rotations I've remembered
traced circles in snow disappeared into white
& in black, spirals on the back of a dream
Forgetting is everywhere
empires have imagined lines
yet I know it by how it wells up in I
in the shade of the mothertree
or winter's scarcity

Imagine circles
Remember, NOW
as if the sun were to abandon tomorrow
as if the birds were to detonate the sky
& the ice were to melt into the sea
Remember, the way winter remembers spring
& the wild foods return the wild in we
Remember what it means to live

www.ingramcontent.com/pod-product-compliance
Lightning Source LLC
Chambersburg PA
CBHW022054080426
42734CB00009B/1340